The 31 Kingdom Declarations
Speak, Establish, and Manifest Your Destiny

A Daily Guide to Spiritual Authority, Purpose, and Generational Impact

Gerard Assey

The 31 Kingdom Declarations: Speak, Establish, and Manifest Your Destiny

By

Gerard Assey

Published by:
Gerard Assey
19/18, Palli Arasan Street
Anna Nagar East
Chennai - 600 102

ISBN: 978-81-69340-37-3

Table of Contents

- ✓ DAY 15: DECLARATION OF HEALTHY, GOD-ALIGNED RELATIONSHIPS
- ✓ DAY 16: DECLARATION OF LEADERSHIP AUTHORITY AND INFLUENCE
- ✓ DAY 17: DECLARATION OF EMOTIONAL STRENGTH AND SELF-MASTERY
- ✓ DAY 18: DECLARATION OF EFFECTIVE COMMUNICATION AND WISDOM IN WORDS
- ✓ DAY 19: DECLARATION OF SERVICE, HUMILITY, AND KINGDOM IMPACT
- ✓ DAY 20: DECLARATION OF KINGDOM IMPACT AND RELEVANCE
- ✓ DAY 21: DECLARATION OF MULTIPLICATION AND REPRODUCTION
- ✓ DAY 22: DECLARATION OF SPIRITUAL AUTHORITY AND DOMINION
- ✓ DAY 23: DECLARATION OF SPIRITUAL DISCERNMENT AND SENSITIVITY
- ✓ DAY 24: DECLARATION OF PRAYER POWER AND SPIRITUAL CONSISTENCY
- ✓ DAY 25: DECLARATION OF DIVINE PROTECTION AND COVERING
- ✓ DAY 26: DECLARATION OF DIVINE TIMING AND SEASONAL ALIGNMENT
- ✓ DAY 27: DECLARATION OF GENERATIONAL BLESSING AND COVENANT LEGACY
- ✓ DAY 28: DECLARATION OF DIVINE REMEMBRANCE AND VISITATION
- ✓ DAY 29: DECLARATION OF GLORY, EXCELLENCE, AND DISTINCTION
- ✓ DAY 30: DECLARATION OF COMPLETION AND FULFILLMENT

PREFACE

Why This Book Exists

There comes a point in life when you realize that many people are not limited by lack of opportunity—but by lack of alignment. They hope, they wish, they pray, they desire… yet their lives remain unchanged. Not because God is unwilling, but because they have not learned how to partner with Him through what they believe, speak, and live.

This book was born out of that realization.

I have seen sincere, faith-filled people struggle—not because they lacked faith in their hearts, but because they lacked consistency in their words and alignment in their actions. They believed one thing internally, spoke another externally, and lived in contradiction daily. That disconnect quietly eroded their progress.

At the same time, I began to observe something powerful: those who consistently declared truth, aligned their thinking, and acted intentionally began to experience tangible shifts. Not overnight magic—but undeniable transformation.

This is where **Kingdom Declarations** come in.

Affirmations vs Kingdom Declarations

There is a difference—and it matters.

Affirmations are often rooted in human desire and self-motivation. They are positive, encouraging, and helpful—but they are limited to what the mind can conceive.

Kingdom declarations, however, are rooted in God's Word, God's authority, and God's intention. They are not just positive statements—they are spiritual alignments.

An affirmation may say: *"I am successful."*

A Kingdom declaration says: *"I walk in the purpose ordained for me, and my life produces fruit according to God's design."*

One is self-generated. The other is scripture-backed, faith-driven, and spiritually enforced.

Declarations are not about pretending something is true—they are about aligning with what is already established in the spirit and bringing it into manifestation.

The Role of Faith, Speaking, and Alignment

Faith is not silent. What you truly believe will eventually show up in:

- ✓ *What you say*
- ✓ *How you think*
- ✓ *What you consistently do*

Declarations work when three things align:

1. Faith (What you believe)
2. Words (What you speak)
3. Actions (How you live)

If these are disconnected, results are limited.

But when they align—there is power.

- ✓ *You begin to think differently.*
- ✓ *You begin to speak with conviction.*
- ✓ *You begin to act with clarity.*

And slowly—but surely—your life begins to shift.

A Personal Observation

There was a season where I noticed something uncomfortable in my own life.

I was saying the right things occasionally—but not consistently. I was believing in possibilities—but entertaining doubt in private. I desired progress—but tolerated habits that worked against me.

Nothing dramatic was wrong—but nothing significant was changing either.

That's when I made a deliberate shift.

I began to speak intentionally every day—not casually, not emotionally, but deliberately. I aligned my words with truth. I removed contradictory speech. I became conscious of my internal dialogue. And more importantly—I began to act in alignment with what I declared. What changed?

Not everything at once. But enough to notice. Enough to continue. Enough to become convinced.

Clarity increased. Confidence grew. Decisions improved. Opportunities began to align.

That was the turning point.

This Book Is Not for Casual Reading This is not a book to skim. This is a **tool to engage with**.

Each declaration is designed to:

- ✓ *Shape your thinking*
- ✓ *Align your identity*
- ✓ *Strengthen your conviction*
- ✓ *Guide your actions*

If you read it casually, you will feel inspired. If you engage with it intentionally, you will be transformed.

Final Thought Before You Begin

You are not reading this by accident.

There is more in you. There is more for you. And there is a way to step into it deliberately.

This book is your guide.

- ✓ *Speak with intention.*
- ✓ *Believe with conviction.*
- ✓ *Live in alignment.*

And watch what begins to change.

INTRODUCTION

The Power of Speaking and Establishing

"You don't become what you wish—you become what you consistently declare and align with."

This is not just a powerful statement—it is a principle of life.

- ✓ *Many people spend years wishing for change:*
- ✓ *"I hope things improve."*
- ✓ *"I wish I had more clarity."*
- ✓ *"I want a better life."*

But wishing is passive.

Life does not respond to wishes. Life responds to **alignment and consistency**.

The Principle of Establishment

Scripture reveals a powerful truth in Job 22:28:

"You shall decree a thing, and it shall be established unto you..."

This is not poetry—it is a principle.

To **decree** means:

- ✓ To declare with authority
- ✓ To speak with intention
- ✓ To establish direction

To **establish** means:

- ✓ To make firm
- ✓ To bring into reality
- ✓ To set into motion

This means your words are not empty—they are **direction-setting forces**.

But here is where many misunderstand this principle:

It is not about saying something once and expecting instant results. It is about ***consistent declaration + internal belief + aligned action***.

How Words Shape Your Life

Your words are not just expressions—they are **constructors**.

They shape three critical areas:

1. Identity *(Who You Become)*

What you consistently say about yourself becomes your internal narrative.

If you repeatedly say:

- ✓ "I am not good enough"
- ✓ "I always struggle"
- ✓ "This is just how I am"

Your mind accepts it. Your behavior follows it.

But when you begin to declare:

"I am growing, learning, and becoming"

"I walk in purpose and clarity"

"I am disciplined and consistent"

Your identity begins to shift.

And once identity shifts—everything else follows.

2. Direction (How You Move)

Words influence decisions.

If your language is:

- ✓ *Fear-based → You hesitate*
- ✓ *Doubt-based → You delay*
- ✓ *Negative → You withdraw*

But when your words are:

- ✓ Faith-filled → You act
- ✓ Clear → You decide
- ✓ Purpose-driven → You move intentionally

Declarations remove internal confusion and create **forward momentum**.

3. Outcomes (What You Experience)

Your outcomes are not random.

They are shaped by:

- ✓ *Your thinking*
- ✓ *Your speaking*
- ✓ *Your actions*

Words influence all three.

When you consistently declare truth, you begin to:

- ✓ *See differently*
- ✓ *Choose differently*
- ✓ *Act differently*

And eventually—you experience differently.

Why Declarations Fail for Some People

Let's be honest. Many people have tried declarations… and seen little result.

Why? Because they:

- ✓ *Said words without belief*
- ✓ *Declared occasionally, not consistently*
- ✓ *Spoke positively but acted negatively*
- ✓ *Used declarations emotionally, not intentionally*

Declarations are not magic phrases.

They are **alignment tools**.

What Happens When You Do This Right

When you:

Speak consistently

Believe intentionally

Act accordingly

Three things begin to happen:

- ✓ *Your thinking becomes structured and focused*
- ✓ *Your confidence increases naturally*
- ✓ *Your life begins to reflect what you are declaring*

Not instantly—but inevitably.

Your Responsibility as You Begin

This book will guide you—but it cannot replace your participation.

- ✓ *You must:*
- ✓ *Speak daily*
- ✓ *Reflect honestly*
- ✓ *Act intentionally*

Do not rush the process.
Do not skip the depth.
Do not treat this lightly.

Final Charge Before You Start

Your words matter.
Your alignment matters.
Your consistency matters.
You are not here to experiment—you are here to transform.

As you go through these 31 days:

- ✓ *Speak with authority.*
  Believe with conviction.
  Act with intention.

And you will not remain the same.

HOW TO USE THIS BOOK

From Reading to Real Transformation

Most people will read a book like this, feel inspired for a few minutes, and then return to old patterns. That will not produce change.

This book is not meant to be read casually—it is meant to be engaged with intentionally.

If you follow the structure below consistently, you will not just feel encouraged—you will experience real, measurable transformation.

DAILY PRACTICE STRUCTURE (Your Non-Negotiable System)

Each day's declaration is designed to be processed in five steps:

1. Read the Declaration Aloud (Morning Activation)

Do not read silently.

Speak it.

Your voice matters. When you speak, you:

- ✓ *Reinforce belief*
- ✓ *Activate focus*

Establish direction for the day

Example:

Instead of reading quietly:

"I walk in divine wisdom…"

Say it aloud with intention:

"I walk in divine wisdom today. I make clear, confident decisions."

Speak slowly. Speak clearly. Speak like you mean it.

2. Personalize It (Make It Real)

Generic statements have limited impact. Personalization creates connection.

Insert:

- ✓ *Your name*
- ✓ *Your current situation*
- ✓ *Your specific need*

Example:

Original: *"I walk in favor."*

Personalized: *"Gerard, you walk in divine favor today—in your meetings, decisions, and interactions."*

If you're facing a challenge:

"I walk in favor in this interview… in this business decision… in this relationship."

Now it becomes real—not theoretical.

3. Meditate on the Scriptures (5–10 Minutes)

Do not rush this step.

Read the scriptures slowly. Reflect on:

- ✓ *What is God saying here?*
- ✓ *What does this mean for me today?*

Example:

If the scripture says, "*The Lord is my shepherd…*"

Pause and ask:

- ✓ *What does it mean for God to guide me today?*
- ✓ *Where do I need direction right now?*

Meditation moves truth from your head → heart → behavior.

4. Reflect (Journal Honestly)

Transformation happens in reflection.

Write briefly:

- ✓ *What stood out to me today?*

- ✓ *Where am I not aligned with this declaration?*
- ✓ *What must change immediately?*

Example:
"I say I am disciplined—but I delay important tasks. Today I must act immediately."
Be honest. This is where growth happens.

5. Act on One Instruction (Daily Execution)
Without action, declarations remain words.
Every day, identify ONE simple action.
Example:
If your declaration is about discipline → Complete one task you've been postponing
If it's about relationships → Call or reconcile with someone
If it's about purpose → Spend 30 minutes working on your calling
Small, consistent actions create massive change.

RECOMMENDED DAILY ROUTINE
To maximize impact, structure your day like this:
Morning: Declaration (5–10 minutes)

- ✓ *Speak the declaration*
- ✓ *Personalize it*
- ✓ *Set intention for the day*

This sets your mental and spiritual direction.

Afternoon: Awareness (Live It)
Stay conscious of your words and actions
Ask: *"Am I living what I declared?"*
Example:

- ✓ *If you declared confidence—don't shrink back in conversations.*
- ✓ *If you declared discipline—don't procrastinate.*

This is where alignment happens.

Night: Reflection (5 minutes)

- ✓ *What did I do well today?*
- ✓ *Where did I fall short?*
- ✓ *What will I improve tomorrow?*

No guilt. Just awareness and adjustment.

REPETITION CYCLE (THE SECRET TO LASTING CHANGE)

Do not stop after 31 days.
Repeat this cycle for 3 months minimum.
Why? Because:

- ✓ *Repetition builds belief*
- ✓ *Belief shapes identity*
- ✓ *Identity drives behavior*

Month 1: Awareness
Month 2: Alignment
Month 3: Transformation
By the third cycle, what felt forced will feel natural.

Final Instruction for This Section

- ✓ Do not rush.
- ✓ Do not skip steps.
- ✓ Do not treat this lightly.

Consistency—not intensity—produces results.

DAY 1:
DECLARATION OF DIVINE HEALTH AND WHOLENESS

I decree and declare that my body is the temple of the Holy Spirit (1 Corinthians 6:19), and therefore sickness, disease, and affliction have no legal right to dwell in me.
I declare that I walk in divine health—not managed health, not temporary relief—but complete wholeness in spirit, soul, and body. For it is written in 3 John 1:2, *"Beloved, I wish above all things that you prosper and be in health, even as your soul prospers."* Therefore, my health is aligned with my spiritual prosperity.

I decree that every system in my body functions in divine order. Every cell, every organ, every function aligns with the perfection of God's design. I reject every report that contradicts the Word of God, for whose report shall I believe? I believe the report of the Lord (Isaiah 53:1).

I declare that by the stripes of Jesus Christ, I am healed (Isaiah 53:5). Healing is not something I am trying to receive—it is something I enforce, because it has already been accomplished.

I command every hidden ailment, every inherited weakness, every attack on my body to be uprooted now. I declare that I am immune to every form of destruction that walks in darkness or wastes at noonday (Psalm 91:6).

I decree vitality, strength, and divine energy. I shall not be weak, I shall not be fatigued, I shall not be broken. The same Spirit that raised Christ from the dead quickens my mortal body (Romans 8:11).
I walk in discipline, wisdom, and stewardship over my body. I make choices that align with life, strength, and longevity.

Meditation Scriptures: Psalm 103:2–3, Isaiah 53:5, Romans 8:11, 3 John 1:2
And it is established.

DAY 2:
DECLARATION OF DIVINE WISDOM AND STRATEGIC INSIGHT

I decree and declare that I operate in divine wisdom—wisdom that is from above, pure, peaceable, and full of good fruits (James 3:17).
I declare that I do not walk in confusion or uncertainty. For God is not the author of confusion (1 Corinthians 14:33), therefore clarity is my portion.
I decree that I have the mind of Christ (1 Corinthians 2:16). I think differently, I see differently, and I discern accurately. I am not led by emotions, pressure, or fear—I am led by divine insight.

As it is written in James 1:5, *"If any of you lack wisdom, let him ask of God..."*—I receive wisdom freely and generously. In every decision I make, wisdom speaks.
I declare that I will not make costly mistakes. I will not take wrong turns. Even when situations appear complex, divine strategy unfolds before me.
I decree that I am ten steps ahead by the Spirit of God. I anticipate challenges, I solve problems, and I walk in solutions.
I declare that kings will seek my counsel, and systems will depend on my insight (Proverbs 8:15–16). I carry answers in a world full of questions.
I walk in understanding of times and seasons (1 Chronicles 12:32). I know what to do and when to do it.

Meditation Scriptures: James 1:5, Proverbs 3:5–6, 1 Corinthians 2:16, James 3:17
And it is established.

DAY 3:
DECLARATION OF SUPERNATURAL PROSPERITY AND SUPPLY

I decree and declare that I walk in covenant prosperity. Lack is not my portion, scarcity is not my reality, and insufficiency has no place in my life.
For it is written in Philippians 4:19, *"My God shall supply all your need according to His riches in glory..."* Therefore, my supply is not from the earth—it is from heaven.
I declare that I am a channel of abundance. Resources flow to me and through me. I do not struggle—I steward.
I decree that the work of my hands is blessed (Deuteronomy 28:12). Every effort I make produces results. Every seed I sow yields a harvest.
I declare open doors of opportunity, multiple streams of income, and divine connections that elevate my financial life.

I reject financial anxiety, fear, and limitation. I walk in confidence, knowing that God is my source.
I decree that I lend and do not borrow (Deuteronomy 28:12). I am a giver, a builder, and a kingdom financier.
I declare that wealth and riches are in my house (Psalm 112:3), not for selfish gain, but for kingdom impact and generational legacy.

Meditation Scriptures: Philippians 4:19, Deuteronomy 28:12, Psalm 112:3, 2 Corinthians 9:8
And it is established.

DAY 4:
DECLARATION OF DIVINE FAVOR AND UNCOMMON ACCESS

I decree and declare that I walk in divine favor that distinguishes me.
As it is written in Psalm 5:12, *"For You, O Lord, will bless the righteous; with favor You will surround him as with a shield."* I am surrounded by favor.
I declare that doors open for me without struggle. Opportunities locate me without striving.
I decree that I am remembered in rooms where my name was forgotten. I am recommended by those who matter.
I declare that favor speaks for me where I cannot speak for myself.

I walk into places I am not qualified for by human standards, but grace qualifies me.
I decree preferential treatment, divine endorsement, and supernatural acceptance.
Men and women go out of their way to bless me, support me, and advance me.

Meditation Scriptures: Psalm 5:12, Luke 2:52, Proverbs 3:4, Genesis 39:21
And it is established.

DAY 5:
DECLARATION OF VICTORY AND DOMINION

I decree and declare that I am more than a conqueror through Christ (Romans 8:37).
I do not fight for victory—I enforce it. Victory is my starting point.
For it is written in 1 Corinthians 15:57, *"Thanks be to God who gives us the victory..."*—therefore, I walk daily in triumph.
I declare that no weapon formed against me shall prosper (Isaiah 54:17).
I decree that every challenge becomes a stepping stone, every opposition becomes an advantage.

I declare dominion over fear, over limitation, and over every negative circumstance.
I rise above every storm. I overcome every obstacle.
I am unstoppable, unshaken, and undefeated.

Meditation Scriptures: Romans 8:37, 1 Corinthians 15:57, Isaiah 54:17, 2 Corinthians 2:14
And it is established.

DAY 6:
DECLARATION OF DIVINE DIRECTION AND CLARITY

I decree and declare that I am led by the Spirit of God in all things.
For it is written in Proverbs 3:5–6, *"Trust in the Lord… He shall direct your paths."* My paths are divinely directed.
I declare that I do not wander, I do not guess—I am guided.
I decree that every step I take is ordered by the Lord (Psalm 37:23).

I hear clearly, I discern accurately, and I act confidently.
I reject confusion, delay, and misalignment.
I walk in precision, purpose, and divine timing.

Meditation Scriptures: Proverbs 3:5–6, Psalm 37:23, Isaiah 30:21, Romans 8:14
And it is established.

DAY 7:
DECLARATION OF COURAGE, STRENGTH, AND RESILIENCE

I decree and declare that I am strong in the Lord and in the power of His might (Ephesians 6:10).
I refuse fear, intimidation, and discouragement.
For it is written in Joshua 1:9, *"Be strong and courageous…"*—therefore, I rise boldly.
I declare that I do not quit, I do not give up, I do not back down.

I endure, I persist, and I overcome.
I decree that pressure does not break me—it builds me.
I am resilient, steadfast, and immovable.
I finish what I start, and I finish strong.

Meditation Scriptures: Joshua 1:9, Isaiah 41:10, Ephesians 6:10, Galatians 6:9
And it is established.

DAY 8:
DECLARATION OF TRUE IDENTITY IN CHRIST

I decree and declare that I know who I am in Christ, and I am firmly established in my divine identity. I am not defined by my past, my failures, my background, or the opinions of people. I am defined by God Himself, the One who created me, called me, and redeemed me for His purpose.

For it is written in 2 Corinthians 5:17, *"If any man be in Christ, he is a new creation…"* Therefore, I declare that I am not a work in progress trying to become—I am already made new. Old limitations, old mindsets, and old identities have passed away. I walk boldly in the newness of life.

I decree that I am chosen, royal, and set apart, according to 1 Peter 2:9. I am not ordinary—I am a royal priesthood, a peculiar person, called to show forth the praises of Him who called me out of darkness into His marvelous light.

I reject every identity crisis, every insecurity, and every comparison. I do not compete, because I am complete in Christ (Colossians 2:10). I am fearfully and wonderfully made (Psalm 139:14), crafted with intentionality and purpose.

I declare that I carry divine DNA. I think like Christ, I respond like Christ, and I reflect Christ in my actions, my words, and my decisions. I am not trying to fit into the world—I am sent to influence it.

I walk with confidence, not arrogance; with assurance, not pride. My identity is anchored, unshakable, and divinely secured.
I declare that I show up as who God says I am—every day, in every place, and in every situation.

Meditation Scriptures: 2 Corinthians 5:17, 1 Peter 2:9, Psalm 139:14, Colossians 2:10
And it is established.

DAY 9:
DECLARATION OF PURPOSE DISCOVERY AND ALIGNMENT

I decree and declare that my life is not accidental—I am here on assignment. I am created with intention, designed with precision, and placed strategically in this generation for a divine purpose.
For it is written in Jeremiah 1:5, *"Before I formed you in the womb, I knew you..."* Therefore, I declare that my purpose is not something I invent—it is something I discover and align with.
I reject confusion about my life's direction. I declare clarity, revelation, and understanding concerning why I am here and what I am called to do.
I decree that every gift, talent, and ability within me is activated and aligned with my purpose. Nothing within me will lie dormant. I am not a reservoir—I am a channel.

I declare that I will not waste time on distractions, misalignments, or pursuits that are not connected to my assignment. I walk with intentionality, focus, and discipline.
I decree that divine connections come into my life—people, mentors, and opportunities that align with my purpose and accelerate my journey.
I declare that I am positioned in the right places at the right time, doing the right things, with the right people.
My life produces impact. My existence carries meaning. My journey fulfills destiny.

Meditation Scriptures: Jeremiah 1:5, Proverbs 19:21, Ephesians 2:10, Romans 8:28

And it is established.

DAY 10:
DECLARATION OF CALLING AND DIVINE ASSIGNMENT

I decree and declare that I am called by God and separated unto a divine assignment. My life is not random—it is commissioned.
For it is written in Romans 11:29, *"The gifts and calling of God are without repentance."* Therefore, I declare that my calling is irrevocable and unstoppable.
I reject every attempt to dilute, distract, or delay my calling. I will not settle for less, shrink back, or abandon what God has entrusted to me.
I decree that I walk boldly in my assignment, even when it is uncomfortable, unfamiliar, or challenging. I am strengthened to carry what I have been called to carry.
I declare that I will not compare my calling with others. I honor my unique assignment, knowing that God has entrusted me with something specific and significant.

I decree that I function with clarity, boldness, and authority. I speak when I must speak, act when I must act, and stand when I must stand.
I declare that my calling produces fruit—visible, tangible, undeniable results that glorify God.
I am not hidden—I am revealed in due time. I am not overlooked—I am positioned.
My life answers a need. My calling solves a problem. My existence fulfills a divine agenda.

Meditation Scriptures: Romans 11:29, 2 Timothy 1:9, Acts 20:24, Galatians 1:15

And it is established.

DAY 11:
DECLARATION OF INFLUENCE AND IMPACT

I decree and declare that I am a person of influence, called to shape environments, impact lives, and transform systems.
For it is written in Matthew 5:14, *"You are the light of the world..."* Therefore, I declare that I do not hide—I shine.
I decree that wherever I go, I bring light, clarity, and transformation. I influence conversations, decisions, and outcomes.
I declare that my voice carries weight. My presence makes a difference. My actions create ripple effects.
I reject insignificance, invisibility, and limitation. I am not small—I am strategic.
I decree that I influence for good, for truth, and for righteousness. I do not manipulate—I impact.
I declare that doors open for me to speak, to lead, and to contribute at higher levels.

I am a voice in my generation. I am a solution in my environment. I am a catalyst for change.
My influence grows, expands, and multiplies.

Meditation Scriptures: Matthew 5:14–16, Genesis 41:39–41, Proverbs 11:11, Acts 1:8
And it is established.

DAY 12: DECLARATION OF DISCIPLINE AND CONSISTENCY

I decree and declare that I am disciplined, focused, and consistent in all that I do.
For it is written in 1 Corinthians 9:27, *"I discipline my body and bring it into subjection..."* Therefore, I declare that I am not controlled by impulses—I am governed by purpose.
I reject procrastination, inconsistency, and distraction.
I decree that I show up daily, faithfully, and intentionally.
I declare that I build habits that produce success, growth, and excellence.

I am not driven by feelings—I am driven by commitment.
I finish what I start. I follow through. I stay the course.
Small steps, done consistently, produce great results in my life.

Meditation Scriptures: 1 Corinthians 9:27, Proverbs 13:4, Galatians 6:9, Hebrews 12:11
And it is established.

DAY 13: DECLARATION OF BOLDNESS AND CONFIDENCE

I decree and declare that I walk in boldness and confidence—not in myself, but in God who strengthens me.
For it is written in Hebrews 4:16, *"Let us therefore come boldly..."* Therefore, I declare that I approach life boldly.
I reject fear, intimidation, and self-doubt.
I decree that I speak with confidence, act with assurance, and lead with clarity.
I declare that I am not ashamed of who I am or what I carry.

I step into rooms with confidence. I take opportunities with boldness. I rise without hesitation.
I am courageous, fearless, and unstoppable.

Meditation Scriptures: Hebrews 4:16, 2 Timothy 1:7, Proverbs 28:1, Acts 4:29
And it is established.

DAY 14:
DECLARATION OF LEGACY AND GENERATIONAL IMPACT

I decree and declare that my life is not just about me—it is about legacy.
For it is written in Proverbs 13:22, *"A good man leaves an inheritance…"* Therefore, I declare that I build beyond my lifetime.
I decree that what I do today impacts generations tomorrow.
I declare that I raise, mentor, and influence others.

I build systems, values, and structures that outlive me.
I am not temporary—I am generational.
My life leaves a mark, a legacy, and a testimony.

Meditation Scriptures: Proverbs 13:22, Psalm 112:1–2, 2 Timothy 2:2, Deuteronomy 7:9
And it is established.

DAY 15:
DECLARATION OF HEALTHY, GOD-ALIGNED RELATIONSHIPS

I decree and declare that my relationships are divinely aligned, life-giving, and purpose-driven. I do not walk in confusion, toxicity, or misalignment in my relationships—whether personal, professional, or spiritual.

For it is written in Amos 3:3, *"Can two walk together unless they agree?"* Therefore, I declare that I am connected to people who align with my values, my calling, and my direction in life.

I reject every relationship that drains, distracts, manipulates, or diminishes me. I discern clearly between divine connections and destructive associations. I do not hold on to what God is asking me to release.

I decree that God brings into my life the right people at the right time—destiny helpers, covenant relationships, wise counselors, and faithful companions.

I declare that I also become the right person in relationships. I walk in love, patience, humility, and truth. I do not just seek value—I add value.

I am slow to anger, quick to listen, and wise in my responses (James 1:19). I speak words that build, heal, and strengthen.

I decree that there is no strife, jealousy, or division in my relationships. Where there has been misunderstanding, clarity comes. Where there has been hurt, healing flows. Where there has been

distance, restoration is established—if aligned with God's will.
I walk in forgiveness. I release offense. I do not carry emotional baggage that limits my future.
I declare that my relationships are a source of strength, joy, growth, and divine acceleration.

Meditation Scriptures: Amos 3:3, Proverbs 13:20, 1 Corinthians 15:33, Colossians 3:13
And it is established.

DAY 16:
DECLARATION OF LEADERSHIP AUTHORITY AND INFLUENCE

I decree and declare that I am called to lead, to influence, and to take responsibility. Leadership is not a title I hold—it is a mantle I carry.

For it is written in Genesis 1:28, *"Be fruitful… have dominion…"* Therefore, I declare that I walk in dominion, not passivity.

I reject timidity, hesitation, and self-doubt in leadership. I rise with confidence, clarity, and conviction.

I decree that I lead with integrity, wisdom, and vision.

I do not lead by control or fear—I lead by example, influence, and inspiration.

I declare that I see ahead, think strategically, and act decisively. I am not reactive—I am proactive.

I decree that people trust my leadership because I walk in truth and consistency. I do not compromise values for convenience.

I declare that I empower others. I do not hoard authority—I develop people. I raise leaders, not followers.

I lead with humility. I am teachable, accountable, and continually growing.

I decree that my leadership produces results—growth, progress, and transformation.

Where I lead, things improve. Where I serve, systems are strengthened. Where I influence, people are elevated.

Meditation Scriptures: Genesis 1:28, Matthew 20:26–28, Proverbs 11:14, 1 Timothy 4:12

And it is established.

DAY 17:
DECLARATION OF EMOTIONAL STRENGTH AND SELF-MASTERY

I decree and declare that I am emotionally strong, stable, and mature. I do not live at the mercy of my feelings—I live under the guidance of the Spirit of God.

For it is written in Proverbs 25:28, *"He that has no rule over his own spirit is like a city broken down…"* Therefore, I declare that I have mastery over my emotions.

I reject anger, impulsiveness, insecurity, and emotional instability.

I decree that I respond with wisdom, not react with emotion. I pause, discern, and act with clarity.

I declare that I am not easily offended, discouraged, or shaken. I am grounded, stable, and anchored.

I manage stress effectively. I release anxiety. I walk in peace that surpasses understanding (Philippians 4:7).

I decree that I handle pressure with grace. I do not break under pressure—I grow through it.

I declare that I am self-aware. I understand my triggers, my strengths, and my growth areas—and I intentionally develop.

I choose joy. I choose peace. I choose maturity.

My emotional life is aligned, balanced, and governed by truth.

Meditation Scriptures: Proverbs 25:28, Galatians 5:22–23, Philippians 4:7, James 1:19–20

And it is established.

DAY 18:
DECLARATION OF EFFECTIVE COMMUNICATION AND WISDOM IN WORDS

I decree and declare that my words carry wisdom, power, and grace. I speak life, truth, and clarity in every situation.
For it is written in Proverbs 18:21, *"Death and life are in the power of the tongue…"* Therefore, I declare that I choose life in my words.
I reject careless speech, negativity, gossip, and destructive communication.
I decree that I speak with purpose and precision. My words build, heal, guide, and influence.
I declare that I listen with understanding. I do not just hear—I discern.
I communicate clearly, confidently, and respectfully.

I know when to speak and when to remain silent (Ecclesiastes 3:7).
I decree that my words open doors, resolve conflicts, and create alignment.
I speak truth in love. I correct with wisdom. I encourage with sincerity.
My voice carries influence. My communication produces results.

Meditation Scriptures: Proverbs 18:21, Colossians 4:6, James 1:19, Ecclesiastes 3:7
And it is established.

DAY 19: DECLARATION OF SERVICE, HUMILITY, AND KINGDOM IMPACT

I decree and declare that I am a servant leader, committed to adding value and making a difference.
For it is written in Mark 10:45, *"The Son of Man came not to be served, but to serve…"* Therefore, I declare that service is my posture.
I reject pride, selfish ambition, and entitlement.
I decree that I serve with excellence, humility, and sincerity.
I declare that I look for opportunities to help, support, and uplift others.

I do not wait to be asked—I take initiative.
I serve in small things and great things with the same heart.
I decree that my service creates impact. Lives are changed, systems are improved, and environments are elevated because I showed up.
I declare that as I serve, I am elevated. As I give, I receive. As I pour out, I am replenished.
My life is not about status—it is about significance.

Meditation Scriptures: Mark 10:45, Philippians 2:3–4, Matthew 5:16, Galatians 5:13
And it is established.

DAY 20:
DECLARATION OF KINGDOM IMPACT AND RELEVANCE

I decree and declare that my life is impactful, relevant, and purposeful in my generation.
For it is written in Acts 13:36, *"David served his generation…"* Therefore, I declare that I serve my generation effectively.
I reject a life of insignificance and irrelevance.
I decree that I solve real problems, meet real needs, and create real value.
I declare that my gifts make room for me (Proverbs 18:16).

I show up where it matters. I contribute where it counts.
I influence industries, communities, and lives.
I decree that my work matters, my voice matters, and my presence matters.
I do not drift through life—I drive purposefully.
My life leaves evidence of impact everywhere I go.

Meditation Scriptures: Acts 13:36, Matthew 5:16, Proverbs 18:16, Daniel 6:3
And it is established.

DAY 21:
DECLARATION OF MULTIPLICATION AND REPRODUCTION

I decree and declare that my life multiplies. I do not remain at one level—I grow, expand, and reproduce. For it is written in Genesis 26:12, *"Isaac sowed... and received a hundredfold..."* Therefore, I declare that I walk in multiplication.
I reject stagnation, limitation, and decline.
I decree that everything I do increases—my influence, my impact, my resources, my effectiveness.
I declare that I reproduce myself in others. I mentor, train, and develop people.

I do not build alone—I build through others.
I create systems that multiply results.
I declare that my life produces fruit that remains (John 15:16).
I move from addition to multiplication in every area.
My impact grows beyond me. My work outlives me.
My influence multiplies across generations.

Meditation Scriptures: Genesis 26:12, John 15:16, 2 Timothy 2:2, Matthew 13:23
And it is established.

DAY 22:
DECLARATION OF SPIRITUAL AUTHORITY AND DOMINION

I decree and declare that I walk in spiritual authority, not as a concept, but as a living reality. I am not powerless, I am not vulnerable—I am empowered by God to rule, to enforce, and to establish His will on the earth.
For it is written in Luke 10:19, *"Behold, I give you authority… over all the power of the enemy…"* Therefore, I declare that I walk in dominion over every force that opposes my life, my purpose, and my destiny.

I reject every mindset of defeat, fear, and helplessness. I am not a victim—I am victorious.
I decree that I take authority over my environment, my circumstances, and every spiritual resistance. I do not beg for change—I command alignment.
I declare that my words carry authority. When I speak in alignment with God's Word, things shift, situations change, and outcomes align.
I decree that I am spiritually alert, discerning, and grounded. I am not ignorant of the enemy's devices (2 Corinthians 2:11).
I declare that I stand firm in truth, clothed in righteousness, walking in faith, and anchored in peace (Ephesians 6:10–18).
I enforce what has already been established in heaven. I do not fight for victory—I manifest it.
My life reflects dominion, authority, and divine control.

Meditation Scriptures: Luke 10:19, Ephesians 6:10–18, 2 Corinthians 2:11, Romans 8:37

And it is established.

DAY 23: DECLARATION OF SPIRITUAL DISCERNMENT AND SENSITIVITY

I decree and declare that I walk in spiritual discernment and sensitivity. I do not walk blindly—I perceive, I understand, and I respond with wisdom.
For it is written in Hebrews 5:14, *"Those who by reason of use have their senses exercised to discern..."* Therefore, I declare that my spiritual senses are sharp and active.

I reject confusion, deception, and misinterpretation.
I decree that I discern times, seasons, people, and situations accurately.
I declare that I hear God clearly. His voice guides me, corrects me, and directs me.
I am sensitive to the Holy Spirit. I do not ignore promptings, I do not override convictions—I respond.
I decree that I recognize opportunities and avoid traps.
I walk in awareness, not assumption. I walk in understanding, not ignorance.
Nothing takes me by surprise. I am prepared, positioned, and perceptive.

Meditation Scriptures: Hebrews 5:14, 1 Kings 3:9, John 10:27, Isaiah 30:21
And it is established.

DAY 24:
DECLARATION OF PRAYER POWER AND SPIRITUAL CONSISTENCY

I decree and declare that I am a person of prayer—consistent, disciplined, and effective.
For it is written in James 5:16, *"The effective, fervent prayer… avails much."* Therefore, I declare that my prayers produce results.

I reject prayerlessness, inconsistency, and spiritual laziness.
I decree that I maintain a strong, active, and growing relationship with God.
I declare that I do not pray out of routine—I pray with intention, faith, and expectation.
I decree that my prayer life strengthens me, aligns me, and empowers me.
I declare that I stand in the gap—for myself, my family, and my generation.
I pray until things shift. I pray until clarity comes. I pray until alignment is established.
I am spiritually consistent, not seasonal.
My prayer life is powerful, productive, and transformative.

Meditation Scriptures: James 5:16, 1 Thessalonians 5:17, Matthew 6:6, Luke 18:1
And it is established.

DAY 25:
DECLARATION OF DIVINE PROTECTION AND COVERING

I decree and declare that I am divinely protected, covered, and secured under the shadow of the Almighty.
For it is written in Psalm 91:1, *"He who dwells in the secret place…"* Therefore, I declare that I dwell in God's presence, and I abide under His protection.

I reject fear, anxiety, and every expectation of harm.
I decree that no evil shall befall me, nor shall any plague come near my dwelling (Psalm 91:10).
I declare that I am preserved in my going out and my coming in (Psalm 121:8).
I decree that I am protected physically, emotionally, spiritually, and mentally.
I declare that every plan of harm is nullified, every trap is exposed, and every attack is dismantled.
I walk in confidence, not fear.
I am covered, secured, and preserved.

Meditation Scriptures: Psalm 91, Psalm 121:7–8, Isaiah 54:17, Proverbs 18:10
And it is established.

DAY 26:
DECLARATION OF DIVINE TIMING AND SEASONAL ALIGNMENT

I decree and declare that I walk in divine timing. I am not early, I am not late—I am aligned.
For it is written in Ecclesiastes 3:1, *"To everything there is a season..."* Therefore, I declare that I function in the right season.
I reject delay, frustration, and misalignment.
I decree that I recognize my season and respond appropriately.
I declare that doors open at the right time, opportunities come at the right moment, and connections happen in divine timing.

I am not rushed, and I am not delayed—I am positioned.
I trust God's timing. I do not force what is not ready, and I do not miss what is prepared.
Everything in my life aligns with divine order.

Meditation Scriptures: Ecclesiastes 3:1, Habakkuk 2:3, Galatians 6:9, Psalm 102:13
And it is established.

DAY 27:
DECLARATION OF GENERATIONAL BLESSING AND COVENANT LEGACY

I decree and declare that I walk in generational blessing, not generational limitation.
For it is written in Deuteronomy 7:9, *"He keeps covenant… to a thousand generations."* Therefore, I declare that my life carries covenant blessings.

I reject every generational curse, pattern, and limitation.
I decree that I break cycles of failure, lack, and dysfunction.
I declare that what flows from me to the next generation is blessing, wisdom, and strength.
I build a legacy of faith, excellence, and impact.
My children and generations after me rise stronger, wiser, and greater.
I am a generational bridge—not a generational barrier.

Meditation Scriptures: Deuteronomy 7:9, Proverbs 13:22, Psalm 112:1–2, Isaiah 59:21
And it is established.

DAY 28:
DECLARATION OF DIVINE REMEMBRANCE AND VISITATION

I decree and declare that God remembers me and visits me with favor, breakthrough, and fulfillment.
For it is written in Genesis 21:1, *"The Lord visited Sarah…"* Therefore, I declare that my season of divine visitation has come.

I reject delay, forgetfulness, and stagnation.
I decree that promises are fulfilled, prayers are answered, and expectations are met.
I declare that what I have waited for manifests.
My time has come. My season has arrived.
I step into fulfillment.

Meditation Scriptures: Genesis 21:1, Luke 1:45, Psalm 106:4, Exodus 3:7
And it is established.

DAY 29:
DECLARATION OF GLORY, EXCELLENCE, AND DISTINCTION

I decree and declare that I walk in glory, excellence, and distinction.
For it is written in Isaiah 60:1, *“Arise, shine…”* Therefore, I declare that I shine.

I reject mediocrity and average living.
I decree that I stand out, excel, and rise above.
I declare that my life reflects God’s glory in every area.
I am distinguished, recognized, and elevated.
Excellence is my standard.

Meditation Scriptures: Isaiah 60:1, Daniel 6:3, Matthew 5:16, Philippians 1:10
And it is established.

DAY 30:
DECLARATION OF COMPLETION AND FULFILLMENT

I decree and declare that I finish what God has started in my life.
For it is written in Philippians 1:6, *"He who began a good work..."* Therefore, I declare completion.

I reject unfinished assignments and abandoned callings.
I decree that I complete my purpose, fulfill my destiny, and finish strong.
Nothing remains incomplete.
My life is fulfilled.

Meditation Scriptures: Philippians 1:6, 2 Timothy 4:7, John 17:4, Hebrews 12:2
And it is established.

DAY 31:
FINAL DECLARATION OF TOTAL ALIGNMENT AND MANIFESTATION

I decree and declare that my life is fully aligned with God's will, purpose, and plan.
For it is written in Romans 8:28, *"All things work together..."* Therefore, I declare total alignment.

Everything in my life—past, present, and future—is working together for good.
I decree manifestation—of promises, of purpose, of destiny.
I declare that I step into fullness, completeness, and abundance.
Nothing is missing, nothing is broken.
I walk in manifestation.
This is my reality.
And it is established.

PERSONAL DECLARATION BUILDER

From Reader to Creator

At some point, you must move beyond using declarations… and begin creating your own.

Why? Because your life is unique.

- ✓ Your challenges are specific.
- ✓ Your calling is personal.

This section equips you to write declarations that are:

- ✓ Scripturally aligned
- ✓ Personally relevant
- ✓ Powerfully effective

THE 4-STEP DECLARATION FORMULA

1. Identity Statement – "I Am…"

Start with who you are becoming.

Examples:

- ✓ *"I am disciplined and focused."*
- ✓ *"I am a person of clarity and purpose."*
- ✓ *"I am growing into a confident and effective leader."*

Identity drives behavior. Always start here.

2. Authority Statement – "I Decree…"

Now speak with authority.

Examples:

- ✓ *"I decree that I act with clarity in every decision today."*
- ✓ *"I decree that fear has no place in my thinking or actions."*

This is not passive—it is intentional.

3. Scripture Anchor
Ground your declaration in truth.
Examples:

- ✓ *"For it is written… I can do all things…"*
- ✓ *"As it is written… God directs my steps…"*

This gives your declaration foundation and confidence.

4. Outcome Statement (What Will Happen)
End with what you expect to see.
Examples:

- ✓ *"Therefore, I make clear decisions and move forward with confidence."*
- ✓ *"As a result, my actions today produce progress and results."*

This creates direction.

FULL EXAMPLE
"I am disciplined and consistent.
I decree that I take immediate action on what matters most.
For it is written that the diligent prosper.
Therefore, I complete my key tasks today with focus and excellence."

Final Instruction

- ✓ Start simple.
- ✓ Write 1–2 personal declarations for areas where you need change.
- ✓ Speak them daily.
- ✓ Live them intentionally.

ACTION PLAN SECTION

Turning Declarations into Real-Life Results
Declarations without action create inspiration—but not transformation.
This section ensures that what you declare becomes what you live.

THE 3-AREA LIFE ALIGNMENT FRAMEWORK
To create balanced growth, focus on three key areas:
1. SPIRITUAL (Your Foundation)
Focus: Connection, clarity, inner strength
Examples:

- ✓ *Daily prayer time (10–15 mins)*
- ✓ *Reading and reflecting on scripture*
- ✓ *Quiet time for thinking and alignment*

2. PERSONAL (Your Discipline & Habits)
Focus: Self-management, consistency
Examples:

- ✓ *Waking up on time*
- ✓ *Completing key tasks daily*
- ✓ *Reducing distractions (phone, social media)*
- ✓ *Building productive habits*

3. EXTERNAL (Your Impact & Results)
Focus: Relationships, work, contribution
Examples:

- ✓ *Improving communication*
- ✓ *Taking initiative at work*
- ✓ *Strengthening relationships*
- ✓ *Adding value to others*

THE START – STOP – CONTINUE METHOD
This is your practical action tool.
1. START (What will I begin doing?)
Example:
- ✓ *Start waking up 30 minutes earlier*
- ✓ *Start planning my day every morning*
- ✓ *Start reaching out to one key person daily*

2. STOP (What must I eliminate?)
Example:
- ✓ *Stop procrastinating on important tasks*
- ✓ *Stop negative self-talk*
- ✓ *Stop wasting time on unproductive habits*

3. CONTINUE (What is already working?)
Example:
- ✓ *Continue daily prayer*
- ✓ *Continue focused work sessions*
- ✓ *Continue learning and improving*

SAMPLE ACTION PLAN (COMPLETE EXAMPLE)
Spiritual:
START: 10 minutes daily reflection
STOP: Skipping quiet time
CONTINUE: Evening prayer
Personal:
START: Completing 3 key tasks daily
STOP: Delaying difficult work
CONTINUE: Morning routine
External:
START: One meaningful conversation daily
STOP: Avoiding tough discussions
CONTINUE: Supporting team members

Final Instruction for This Section
Do not overcomplicate this.
Small, consistent actions:

- ✓ Done daily
- ✓ Aligned with your declarations
- ✓ Repeated over time

...will produce visible, lasting change.

Closing Thought
Declarations set direction. Action creates movement.
Consistency produces results.
Do both—and your life will not remain the same.

FINAL CHARGE / PROPHETIC SEND-OFF

You Have Declared—Now You Must Become
You have not come this far to remain the same.
You have not spoken these words to return to old patterns.
You have not aligned your thoughts to go back into confusion.
You have not awakened your spirit to settle into mediocrity.
This is your line of separation.

You Are Not Ordinary—You Are Commissioned
You are not here by accident.
You are not random.
You are not insignificant.
You are intentional, positioned, and commissioned.
There is something your life must carry.
There is something your voice must release.
There is something your presence must change.
Stop thinking small.
Stop explaining yourself down to fit into spaces you have outgrown.
Stop tolerating what you were designed to transform.
You are not trying to become—you are stepping into what has already been established for you.

Do Not Return to Old Patterns.
This is where many fail.
They experience clarity… and then return to comfort.
They feel conviction… and then go back to convenience.
They declare boldly… and then live casually.

That must not be your story.
Do not go back to:
Inconsistent thinking
Careless speech
Undisciplined living
Misaligned relationships
You have seen too much. You know too much. You have declared too much. Returning is no longer an option.

Live What You Have Declared
Your words have set direction—now your life must follow.
If you declared discipline—be disciplined.
If you declared clarity—make decisions.
If you declared courage—take action.
If you declared purpose—move with intention.
Do not wait for motivation. Do not wait for perfect conditions.
Act now.
Act daily.
Act consistently.
Because transformation does not come from what you say once—it comes from what you live repeatedly.

You Are Now Responsible
This is where ownership begins.
You can no longer say:
"I don't know what to do."
"I'm waiting for the right time."
"Maybe one day…"
No.
You know what to do.
You know how to think.

You know how to speak.
You know how to act.
Now you must choose.

Expect Resistance—But Do Not Yield

As you step forward, expect:

- ✓ *Discomfort*
- ✓ *Doubt*
- ✓ *Resistance*
- ✓ *Distraction*

This is normal.
Anything that grows will be resisted.
Anything that rises will be challenged.
But hear this clearly:

- ✓ *You are not fragile.*
- ✓ *You are not easily shaken.*
- ✓ *You are not easily stopped.*

Stand your ground.
Stay consistent.
Keep moving.

You Will See Results

Not by chance.
Not by luck.
But by alignment.
As you continue:
Your thinking will sharpen
Your confidence will increase
Your decisions will improve
Your results will follow
What once felt difficult will become natural.
What once felt forced will become your identity.

This Is Not the End—This Is Your Beginning

Do not close this book and move on.

- ✓ *Repeat it.*
- ✓ *Revisit it.*
- ✓ *Reinforce it.*
- ✓ *Live it.*

Because this is not just a 31-day journey— This is a new way of thinking, speaking, and living.

Final Declaration

Say this—out loud, with conviction:

“I am not the same.
I think differently.
I speak with intention.
I act with discipline.
I live in alignment.
I do not go back.
I move forward.
I rise.
I become.
And it is established.”

Now go.
Not to try.
Not to experiment.
But to live what you have declared.

About the Author
'GERARD ASSEY'

Gerard Assey is a Graduate in Economics, a PGD in Management (HRD) and holds a Doctorate in Leadership. Gerard holds several International Qualifications in Sales, Debt Collection, Training & Teaching, and is a 'Fellow' of the prestigious 'Institute of Sales & Marketing Management'-UK, a Certified NLP Practitioner, a 'Certified Trainer', an 'Accredited Management Teacher-Behavioral Sciences', a 'Certified Competency Facilitator', a 'Certified Management Consultant'- (the International credentials of a professional management consultant, awarded in accordance with global standards of the ICMCI); and a Certification from the University of Michigan in 'Successful Negotiation: Essential Strategies and Skills'

He is also a Member of the 'National Association of Sales Professionals' backed with several years experience in varied industries, both in India and Overseas. He also holds an 'Etiquette Consultant' Certification from the USA (by Sue Fox, Author of Best Seller: 'Business Etiquette for Dummies'. She has trained some of the top celebrities' world over). He was also a recipient of a scholarship for extensive training in Japan on 'Corporate Management for India'.

Gerard Assey is 'Founder & Chief Corporate Trainer' of the Group: **'Citius, Altius, Fortius Unlimited'**- an organization that **celebrated 20 years of Glorious Service** in 2021, focusing on 3 Core Competencies:

People. Performance. Profit; in functional areas of Sales & Marketing, HR & Organizational Development, covering Recruitment, Training & Consultancy!

Having managed organizations with large Sales Forces in India & Overseas, his specialization cover extensive areas of Sales Training (All levels - Presentation, Negotiation, Key/ Strategic Accounts Management & Managerial Skills for all sectors), Bid Proposal/ Capture Planning/ Management Trainings, Retail Sales, Customer Service & Customer Retention Programs, Training for Prevention & Collection of Debt, Self & Personal Development Programs (Time Management, Teamwork & Team Building, Business Etiquette & Personal Grooming, Leadership & Managerial Skills, People Management Skills, Train-the-Trainer etc), including preparation of Custom-designed Business Manuals for Internal (HR, Induction, and Sales etc) & External use (Instruction, User Manuals).

Gerard has successfully conducted over 6525 Trainings & Workshops (as of May '26) all across India, Middle East, Africa, Europe & S.E. Asia. Besides public programs conducted regularly, both in India & Overseas, he has some of the top names as clients whom he services from Single Owners to large Public & Government undertakings, covering all sectors, for their in-house needs.

His website: www.CollectionSkills.com is the only one in this part of the world to be featured in the 'Collections & Credit Risk Magazine-USA' under 'Who's Who in Training' and ranks TOP, along with other websites listed below on most search engines.

Gerard is author of 230 Books already (May 2026), all the books being available on all online platforms and outlets as E-books and Paperbacks

A few of our business related books:

1. Bite-sized Bits on Commonsense Management
2. Heart to Heart on Life's Principles'
3. How to become a Successful Manager
4. The Sales Professionals' Master Workbook of S.Y.S.T.E.M.S
5. The Professional Business Email Etiquette Handbook & Guide
6. The Professional Business Video-Conferencing Etiquette Handbook & Guide
7. Professional Presentation Skills
8. Exceptional Customer Service
9. Professional Tele-Marketing Skills
10. Professional Debt Collection Skills
11. The G.R.E.A.T. Sales & Service Workbook
12. Sales Training Advantage for Results (*The Ultimate Sales Training Manual to enable you stand out as a S.T.A.R.*)
13. CEO Daily Planner & Organizer
14. The Sales Professionals' Master Daily Planner
15. The Professional Debt Collector's Master Daily Planner
16. My Daily Planner & Organizer
17. MY EMERGENCY INFORMATION RECORD (Family Emergency & Peace of Mind Planner)
18. The Ultimate Therapist & Counselors Planner and Organizer
19. Building an Ethical Workplace
20. Managing Relationships at Work
21. Managing Business Meetings Effectively
22. Effective Delegation Skills
23. Goal Setting for Success
24. B2B Selling by Email
25. Professional Business Etiquette & Grooming
26. Dining Etiquette & Table Manners
27. Effective Networking Skills
28. Grooming, Etiquette & Manners for Teens, Young Adults & Future Leaders
29. Inter-Personal Skills
30. Get Ready, Get Hired!
31. Selling in a Recession
32. Effective Receivables Management in an Economic Downturn!

33. Real Estate & Property Sales Training
34. Credit Sales & Accounts Receivable Management
35. Selling Skills for Real Estate & Property Advisors
36. Take G.R.E.A.T. C.A.R.E!
37. Spa, Salon & Health Club Selling Skills
38. Selling Travel, Holiday & MICE Services
39. Selling Skills for Spa's, Salons & Health Clubs
40. Retailing in Salons & Spas
41. Selling Holiday, Vacation, Tours & Packages
42. The Power of Sales Referrals
43. Selling Luxury
44. Technical Selling Skills
45. Financial Advisors Sales Training
46. Dealing with Burnout at Work Monopolize Your Markets
47. Selling to Affluent Customers
48. Growing up with Grace
49. Financial Selling Skills
50. *The Effective Manager's Guide: Key Skills to Thrive*
51. From Aspiring to Inspiring: A Guide for New Managers on the Rise
52. The Power of Focus
53. Selling with Integrity: Sell Like Jesus The Perfect Role Model!
54. 31 Habits of Champions: Your 31-Day Journey to Greatness
55. Rejecting Grasshopper Talk: From Grasshopper to Giant-Killer-*Defeating Giants Daily!*
56. Navigate the AI-Powered Future of Bid & Proposals: Up-Skill to Stay Relevant with Alternative Career Paths & Opportunities
57. Hiring Sales Winners
58. Present with Impact
59. Success Unlocked: *Breaking Free from Habits that Hold You Back*
60. Complaints to Cheers, Feedback to Gold: Mastering Complaints Management
61. Thriving Together: *Cultivating Diversity, Equity, and Inclusion*
62. Coaching Skills for Sales Managers
63. Soaring to Success in Business & Leadership: Swifter, Higher, Stronger!
64. From Classroom to Podium: A Student's Guide to Powerful Public Speaking & Presentation Skills
65. Developing Self-Discipline

66. The CEO's 31-Day Power Plan: Unlocking Success through Essential Traits
67. Credibility Matters
68. A Winning Attitude
69. Bid & Proposal Management Using AI
70. Sales Forecasting: A Practical & Proven Guide to Strategic Sales Forecasting
71. Elevate & Energize: *50 Dynamic & Fun Activities for Peak Workplace Morale*
72. 'Sales SOS! Sales on Fire! *30 Days to Conquer Chaos & the Nightmares of Success!'*
73. Mastering Sales Managerial Skills: *Building High-Performing Teams & Driving Exceptional Results*
74. Eagle-Eyed Leadership: Unleashing the Power of 31 Lessons from Eagles
75. The Ultimate Employee Training Guide: *Training Today, Leading Tomorrow*
76. Being More Accountable at Work
77. Creating a Culture of Continuous Improvement
78. Effective Questioning & Listening Skills
79. The Power of Value Selling
80. The Growth Mindset
81. Mastering Professional Help Desk Skills
82. The Power to Lead with Empathy
83. Being Prepared: The Key to Unlocking Success
84. Youthful Spark-Youth Energizers, Activities and Games-Igniting the Fun in Youth
85. Ignite your Motivation for Success
86. Elevate Your Executive Presence: *Your Roadmap to Executive Excellence*
87. Smart Decisions: *Mastering Problem Solving with Strategic Solutions for Business Success*
88. Strategic Planning: *Developing and Implementing Strategic Plans to Achieve Long-Term Business Goals*
89. The Power of Stay Interviews
90. Developing G.R.I.T.
91. Adaptability
92. Diagnosis- *A Key Skill for Leadership*
93. The Burnout-Proof Salesperson: *The Master Guide to Preventing Stress & Burnout*- Strategies for Thriving in Sales
94. Learning from Failure: *Keys to Success*
95. Customer Success Management
96. Overcoming the Killers of Motivation

97. The C-Suite Code: *Mastering Skills for Executive Excellence'*
98. Dealing with Difficult Customers
99. Unlocking Your Potential: Mastering the Top 20 Life Skills for a Brighter Future
100. Nurturing Tomorrow's Leaders: *Essential Soft Skills Every Child Must Learn*
101. Lively & Fun Party Games for Seniors & Elders
102. Role Playing for Sales Champions: From Practice to Performance
103. Fun and Exciting Party Games for Kids
104. Case Studies for Sales
105. Role-Playing for Unbeatable Customer Service
106. Case Studies in Customer Service
107. Case Studies in Winning Negotiations
108. Case Studies in Management & Leadership
109. Case Studies in Human Resources & Talent Management
110. CEO Success Blueprint: The Essential Toolkit for CEOs and C-Level Executives
111. The Salesperson's Self-Coaching Guide: *Master Your Own Self-Coaching Plan for Success*
112. Overcoming Procrastination: *Your Ultimate Guide to Stop Delaying and Start Living Your Best Life*
113. When True Colors Are Exposed: *The Journey to Unmasking Humanity*
114. Life-Changing Habits for Teens: Teen Success Blueprint for a Bright Future
115. Workplace Stress-Free: *Proven Strategies to Thrive at Work and Beyond*
116. Objection Overruled: *The Ultimate Guide to Turning 'No' into 'Yes'*
117. Building Strong Teams: *A Comprehensive Guide to Team Building*
118. Ethical & Moral Leadership in Business: *Eliminating Unethical Practices & Building a Culture of Trust & Integrity*
119. Rising Strong: Building Positive: High Self-Esteem for a Fulfilling Life-*A Practical Guide for Students, Employees, Leaders & Entrepreneurs*
120 The Cheerful Mindset: Cultivating a Joyful Outlook Everyday
121. Leading Through Crisis: Case Studies on Crisis Management
122. Selling Beyond the Algorithms

123. MAGEN CAPD- Dialysis Record Journal
124. The Human Side of Healing: *A Master Manual on Professionalism, Patient Experience & Compassionate Care-From Treatment to Trust For Doctors, Nurses & Healthcare Teams*

From the Ministry side, Gerard graduated in the very first batch of Charis Bible College-India & had for over 9 years served as a Part-time Faculty at Charis Bible College-Chennai (Andrew Wommack Ministries-Colorado, USA).
He also holds a Diploma in Worship (a subject closest to his heart) from the JSOW and is also a graduate of the Advanced Mentorship Program (AMP) and the Circle Of Ministerial Engagement (C.O.M.E.) of Prophet Jerome Fernando and a Spiritual Son of the Esteemed Prophet.
An accomplished author of several Secular & Christian Books, Gerard has been on the board of a few international organizations and boasts of being the SON of the MOST HIGH GOD: An ordinary guy following an extraordinary GOD!

...And some of his most recent Christian Books being:

1. A Bouquet of Praises for My KING
2. Christian Jokes for the Serious Religious' Folks!
3. Jesus Healed You!
4. Praise24Ever! (also in Tamil version)
5. The 5G Network of GOD
6. Building Faith over F.E.A.R- FACE EVERYTHING AND RISE with JESUS
7. Hebrew and Greek Praise and Worship Words
8. Godly Mothers' and Grandmothers' Bible Story time for Kids!
9. Miracles of Jesus in Pictures
10. Raise your Praise all 365 Days
11. Thanking GOD with an Attitude of Gratitude
12. Meditating on the Attributes of GOD
13. Puppet Scripts
14. Alcohol Ruins, JESUS Reforms, Renews & Restores!
15. Habakkuk 2:2 Christian Daily Journal, Planner & Organizer
16. ABC of GOD's Word for Handwriting Practice
17. Daily Bible Verse Handwriting Practice (Building Godly Character & Faith through Cursive Handwriting Practice!)
18. Guiding Light: Fun & Faith-Building Bible Activities for Children

19. Rejecting Grasshopper Talk: From Grasshopper to Giant-Killer-*Defeating Giants Daily!*
20. Teen Titans of Faith: *Building Courage, Determination & Christ-like-Esteem*
21. I AM Empowered: *Unleashing Divine Power with Positive Declarations*
22. Be A Solution Provider-*From Passion to Purpose: A Biblical Guide to Being the Answer to the World!*
23. Miracles of JESUS
24. Parables of Jesus for a Meaningful Life!
25. A Grateful Heart: Importance of Sharing Testimonies of GOD's Grace
26. Melodies of Worship to JESUS: 31 Songs of Praise & Worship From My Heart to HIS!
27. I AM SO BLESSED!
28. My Daily Cup of Energizer
29. 31 Leadership Lessons *from* Jesus- *The Supreme Leader*
30. Peace Amidst Storms: A Biblical Guide to Conquering S.T.R.E.S.S.
31. Rise Above: 20 Biblical Eagle Lessons for Life's Triumphs
32. Godly Goal Setting: *The FAITHFUL Blueprint for a Purpose-Driven Life*
33. The Profound Attributes of our Mighty GOD: Understanding the 10S's of the Almighty
34. Worship Now, Worship Forever: *A Journey from Earthly Praise to Eternal Glory*
35. Unceasing Praise & Worship: *365 Days to Worship the King*
36. The ROAR Within: *Living with Purpose and Authority through the Power of the Holy Spirit*
37. From Potential to Purpose: Unlocking and Multiplying Your Talents & Gifts for Kingdom Impact
38. Songs from the Heart: *Worshipping GOD in Your Own Tune & Melody*
39. Awakening Praise & Worship: Hebrew & Greek Words to Raise Your Praise
40. Sing a NEW Song to the LORD Everyday: *Daily Devotions of Praise & Worship to Lift Your Heart & Glorify HIS Name*
41. *The* A.R.O.M.A. of True Worship: *Creating Worship That Delights God*
42. Becoming A Kingdom Champion: *Embracing God's Call for a Life of Purpose & Victory*
43. The Busy Businessman's Daily Devotional: 366 Crisp Truths to Start Your Day Strong
44. The Teacher's Heart: *Daily Devotions for Educators*

45. Anchored! *A 31-Day Devotional for Students Facing Life's Challenges*
46. Suddenly! Unlocking Unorthodox Breakthroughs through Unusual Worship
47. Overcoming Adversity: *Lessons from the Bible for Modern Challenges*
48. LORD, Don't do it without me
49. Kingdom Leadership: *Biblical Principles for Modern Leaders*
50. Heartprints of God- *Growing God's Way:* Daily Devotions for Kids to Shine Bright
51. Send Judah First: Let your Praises Go up First to See the Mighty Move of GOD
52. DIVINE MOMENTS: *Recognizing, Embracing, Preparing, and Walking into Life-Changing Encounters with God*
53. Be a Builder in the Kingdom: *The C.E.M.E.N.T. Guide to Creating a Lasting Legacy*
54. Unshakable: *Pillars of Godly Womanhood* (Pillars of Faith That Changed History)
55. Lead Like a Shepherd: *14 Essential Traits for Pastoral Excellence*
56. The Worship Leader's Arsenal: *Powerful Exhortations to Ignite Thanksgiving, Praise & Worship*
57. Women of UnShakable Faith: *31-Day Devotional for Strength, Purpose & Influence*
58. Called to Teach: *A Complete 10-Week Training Guide for Impactful VBS Teachers*
59. Strumming for the KING: Cowboy Songs of Faith & Fire
60. The Ultimate Youth Camp Playbook: *50 Bible-Centered Indoor Games to Engage, Equip, and Empower Teens*
61. Glad in HIS Presence: *David's Revelation of GOD's Love & Mercy*
62. The Spirit Behind the Sound: *52 Devotionals for Worship Teams*
63. THE COWBOY'S COMPASS: *Riding the Trail of Faith with Grit & Grace*
64. Worship as My Weapon: *Living Victoriously through the Power of Praise*
65. A Worshipper Always Wins*: Living a Life of Victorious Worship*
66. Worship That Leads to the Throne: *Practical Strategies for Worship Leaders to Inspire Their Team & Usher People into God's Presence*

67. Worship as Warfare: *Conquering through the Sound of Surrender*
68. Watchmen on the Walls: *A 31-Day Devotional for Worship Teams*
69. KINGDOM BUSINESS: *52 Biblical Principles for GODLY Leadership & Wise Decisions*
70. From Evening to Morning: *Rediscovering GOD's Sacred Hours*
71. Waves of Glory: *Worship through Dance, Flags, Staff & Sound*
72. WORSHIP TEAM BUILDER: *Guiding Your Team from Formation to Fruitfulness*
73. The Worship Leader's Master Training Manual
74. Skits for the King: Children's Plays for Every Church Occasion
75. Unbreakable: Building Strong Marriages and Families God's Way *(From Vows to Victory)*
76. Songs for my King: *A 31-Day Journey of Praise*
77. Building Powerful Children: *Raising a Generation That Will Shape the Future for God*
78. Character Before Chords: *The Heart of the True Worshipper*
79. 365 Days Before His Throne: A Worshipper's Daily Declarations
80. Broken to Built: *How GOD Restores Lives, Heals Hearts & Uses Broken People for HIS Glory*
81. Fear Did Not Come from God: *Discerning the Source, Dismantling the Stronghold & Walking in Power, Love & a Sound Mind*
82. THE GOD OF BEGINNINGS: *Positioning Your Life for What God Is About to Start*
83. HEALED ALREADY: IT IS FINISHED! Receiving What the Cross Has Completed!
84. A.D.D.E.D. Y.E.A.R.S. When God Overrules the Clock, the Diagnosis, and the Final Word
85. HALLELUJAH -The Sound That Heaven Understands *(Building a Life of Pure Praise)*
86. Worship in the Marketplace, Worship Beyond the Walls: *(Turning Work into Worship)*
87. ALPHA & OMEGA: *Living Secure Between the Beginning and the End*
88. JOYFUL NOISE: When Sound Becomes a Spiritual

Statement (When Heaven Responds to the Sound of Faith)

89. F.A.V.O.R.: Five Dimensions of Divine Advantage
90. THE UNBROKEN LAMB: The B.O.N.E.S. of Divine Precision
91. YOU ARE A WEAPON: Unlocking the Power of Worship That Breaks Chains and Opens Heaven
92. M.A.G.N.I.F.Y. *Seeing God as He Truly Is—and Living Above Everything Else*
93. THE HEALING COVENANT: *God's Provision for Healing, Health, and Restoration of the Whole Body*
94. THE DEEP: *Unlocking the Hidden Supply of God Within You*
95. A Mother's Prayer: *The Hidden Power That Shapes Generations*
96. The 31 Kingdom Declarations: Speak, Establish, and Manifest Your Destiny

Besides regularly contributing to business & trade journals, including international ones such as the 'Creative Training Techniques' and the 'Sales News' of the U.S.A, He is also a member of several prestigious bodies & trade associations, having participated in many Conferences & Workshops in India & Overseas.

Prior to his last assignment of leading & managing a large MNC as head, Gerard had a 3-year stint in the Middle East as a Consultant with a leading British Consultancy Firm.

As the past 'Official Country Representative' for the International Business Award- 'THE STEVIES'-(the business world's own Oscar) for about 4 years- he ensured a few Indian companies that qualify for the same every year!

Gerard can be contacted at:

Email: training@Sales-Training.in,training@CollectionSkills.com
Websites:

www.Sales-Training.in
www.EtiquetteWorks.in
www.CollectionSkills.com
www.RetailSalesTraining.in
www.SalesTrainingIndia.com
www.ManualPreparation.com
www.TrainingWithPuppets.com
www.FirstContactAcademy.com
www.SalesAndMarketingRecruiter.com

www.ingramcontent.com/pod-product-compliance
Ingram Content Group UK Ltd.
Pitfield, Milton Keynes, MK11 3LW, UK
UKHW021341190726
13845UKWH00027B/665

9 788169 340373